SUPER COO

THE NOT BAD ANIMALS

SOPHIE CORRIGAN

Frances Lincoln
Children's Books

Featured Creatures

Spider	6	Wolf	46
Black cat	10	Ant	50
Vampire bat	14	House mouse	54
Sharks	18	Moth	58
Hyena	22	Fox	62
Skunk	26	Toad	66
Vulture	30	Bull	70
Rat	34	Weasel	74
Wasp	38	Crocodile	78
Snake	42	Pigeon	82

Camel	86	Scary dogs	126
Scorpion	90	Earthworm	130
Creepy birds	94	Komodo dragon	134
Killer whale	98	Pig	138
Jellyfish	102	Squid	142
Dung beetle	106	Seagull	146
Centipede	110	Snapping turtle	150
Slug	114	Tasmanian devil	154
Anglerfish	118	Glossary	158
Opossum	122		

Listen up, humans!

We've heard you talking about us animals, and we know that you've been giving us a BAD reputation! You say that we're spooky and ugly and creepy and crawly and icky and ewwy and downright gross. But these are rumors and they're just plain MEAN.

NOT a devil

NOT SWEATY

MUCH TOO CUTE

We're here to set the record straight because we're fed up with the lies you've been spreading.

WIGGLY RIGHTS

I AM BEAUTIFUL

WONDER OF NATURE

GREAT ROOM-MATE

Did you know that spiders are basically superheroes? The little hairs on their legs allow them to stick to walls, and relative to its weight, spider silk is five times stronger than steel.

Or how about the fact that moths help pollinate lots of beautiful flowers to help them bloom and make seeds?

I bet you didn't know that some pigeons are even war heroes. Their sense of direction is so good that they were used to carry messages during World War I and II!

So you see, we're NOT bad animals at all.
We're just misunderstood!

At nighttime, I crawl on your face and sometimes you SWALLOW me. In fact, you swallow about eight of us EVERY YEAR!

Can I join you?

You're never more than a few feet away from me or one of my spider pals. That's right—we're EVERYWHERE.

YES.
ON PURPOSE.

Basically, I'm terrifying. Now excuse me, I have some more butt-weaving to do.

That's all NONSENSE!

I'm more frightened of YOU than you are of ME (and with good reason—I don't want to get squished!).

You don't swallow me. I'd be a very silly spider if I got that close to your mouth. Besides, that's just WEIRD.

Why on Earth would I want to crawl around your hair? I need to be free to stretch my many spidery legs.

Only half of my kind spin webs, and we really, REALLY don't want you to get stuck in them! We make them so we can catch our dinner. When you break them, we have to start all over AGAIN.

Nobody likes to miss a meal.

8

See how cool I am!

Please don't judge me for being a bit hairy...

FACTS:

* There are over 40,000 species of spider in the world, and almost all of them have eight legs and eight eyes. That's a lot of digits and lenses!

* Spiders are not actually insects. They're a type of arachnid, which means they're in the same family as scorpions, ticks, and mites.

* The little hairs on their legs allow them to climb walls and walk on glass— talk about a superpower!

* Spiders are SO good for the environment. They eat bugs, recycle their own webs by eating them, and are a vital food source for birds, frogs, lizards, and even other spiders.

I have many legs to help me scurry around adorably!

I'm actually really cute. Check out my darling little spider paws.

GULP!

I'm not everywhere! I'm too busy catching bugs to hang out in the same places as you.

Webs are way more COOL than creepy. We weave them using silk that is super STRONG. Did you know that relative to its weight, spider silk is five times stronger than steel?

9

ME? SCARY?
You must be joking!

FACTS:

* Did you know that cats can rotate their ears 180 degrees and that their hearing is five times better than a human's?

* Cats are super flexible, which makes them great at catching things. They can even jump up to seven times their own height—wow!

* Meow, meow, meow? Apparently, cats developed meowing just to communicate with humans, and it's rare that they meow at other cats.

* Cats love snoozing—who doesn't? It's thought that domestic cats sleep for about 70% of the day and spend 15% of the day grooming themselves.

I only hiss and spit when I'm SCARED. I meow way more often, which means I'm just looking for a bit of attention.

I promise I'm not picking your favorite things to scratch on purpose. My claws grow quickly, and I need to keep them in tip-top condition somehow.

I act very CUTE and SILLY if you give me catnip.

Why not get me a scratching post to help save your furniture?

Balls of yarn are BRILLIANT!

I might scratch you ACCIDENTALLY when we're playing…Sorry—I just get too excited!

I'm a VAMPIRE BAT

The CLUE'S in the NAME.

I come out on the SPOOKIEST of nights and can see you in the dark.

Screeeeeeeeech!

I communicate by SCREECHING! It's such a pretty sound.

My FAVORITE thing to do is get TANGLED UP in your hair. WHILE YOU'RE ASLEEP.

I use ECHOLOCATION to help me navigate. This means I send out SOUND WAVES (sweet little noises) that echo when they hit an object— how COOL is that?

Don't JUDGE me by my name! Why not call me a "leaf-nosed bat" instead? Or, even better, why not use my Latin name, *Desmodus rotundus*? You can call me Desmond for short.

I have CUTE little clingy hands!

I'm FLUFFY like a nighttime sky puppy.

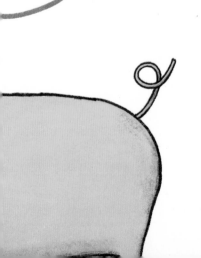

FACTS:

* Vampire bats have a heat sensor on their nose to help them detect warm blood.

* They have "draculin" in their saliva, which keeps the blood flowing while they feed. But don't worry, they don't drink enough blood to harm the animal, just enough to fill their hungry bellies.

* Not at all like Count Dracula, vampire bats are actually social and caring creatures. They live in groups called "colonies" containing between 100 and 1,000 bats and live in warm, dark, and cozy caves.

* Baby vampire bats don't feed on blood, but drink milk produced by their moms.

We are SHARKS

We're silent movers.
You won't hear us coming as we lurk
our way through the water...
UNTIL IT'S TOO LATE!

I'm a GREAT WHITE.
Don't mess with me—I'm a
MENACE! I'm so DEADLY
that they make horror
movies about me.

BOO!

I'm a spine-chilling GOBLIN SHARK. Yes, you heard me—GOBLIN. My name is enough to frighten the living daylights out of anyone.

We LOVE to GOBBLE UP your boats!

EEK!

I'm a HAMMERHEAD. Watch out or I'll use my head to bash and thrash.

We INFEST waters!

There's nothing we like more than skulking around in murky water, looking for humans.

We are the most FEARED creature in the deep blue sea.

That's just RIDICULOUS!

I put the GREAT in great white! I'm the top predator in ocean food chains and help keep a healthy balance of life—and a healthy ocean means a healthy planet.

Sure, there's a GOBLIN shark...

But there's also an ANGEL shark!

I even have little holes on the end of my snout to help me find my dinner.

They pick up the electric currents given off by my prey.

I think you look beautiful!

I'm an aquatic CUTIE and undeniably one of the most AWESOME critters around!

You're more likely to be killed by a
LIGHTNING STRIKE—or a toaster!

FACTS:

* Incredibly, sharks can only swim forward! This is because their fins can't bend in a way that would allow them to move backward.

* Sharks are absolutely ancient and have been on the Earth for at least 450 million years. That's much, MUCH longer than humans have!

* Sharks have amazingly thick skin. This is to keep them warm and to support all of their super-strong muscles. (It also means insults don't bother them.)

* Aside from humans, great white sharks are at the top of the food chain, which means they're not under threat from any other creature.

My fins are
POINTY.

How cool is that?

Whale sharks don't even HAVE teeth, so there's no need to be scared of them.

Plus—they're
POLKA-DOT!

Hi!

I'm a HYENA

I'm a spotted hyena, and I'm a horrible, dirty scavenger. I'm ready to steal anything at a moment's notice!

I'm sneaky, sly, AND stinky... and I LIKE it!

My fur is ALWAYS dirty. I attract flies, and don't even care.

I have a big, bloated potbelly from all the food I've stolen. Delicious!

HA! Don't make me LAUGH!

I'm actually really SMART. Smarter than a chimpanzee, in fact!

Have you seen my EXCELLENT mohawk? Completely awesome.

I think you'll agree, I'm pretty cute too. Just LOOK at my huge, fluffy ears.

I know it might seem like it, but I'm really not laughing at a private joke. In fact, the truth is no laughing matter.

The GIGGLING noise I make means I'm FRUSTRATED, EXCITED, or SCARED.

I'm absolutely not a scavenger, OR lazy. Almost 50% of the food I eat, I catch myself.

I'm a VERY interesting creature!

FACTS:

*   There are three species of hyena, but the spotted hyena is the most common and mostly lives in sub-Saharan Africa.

*   Spotted hyenas are very social creatures and live in large groups called clans, which can have up to 130 hyenas in them.

*   Spotted hyena clans are led by one powerful female hyena. Girl power!

*   Spotted hyenas make lots of different noises to communicate with each other, including yells, whoops, and cackles, which often sounds like they're giggling!

Teamwork makes the dream work!

Got any leftovers?

LIONS are actually more likely to steal food from ME!

I'm a SKUNK

I make the worst smell you can imagine...worse than eggs gone bad or sour milk or your little brother's stinky diaper. And I'm not even sorry!

And if you get in the way of my spray, I'll make you smell bad FOREVER!

My tail is SO HORRIBLY hairy, you can't miss it.

It's my mission to destroy all sweet-smelling plants with my foul-smelling butt.

Give me a BREAK!

OK, it's true that my butt doesn't necessarily smell of roses—but I bet yours doesn't either.

Sorry if I accidentally built my home near yours! I try to mind my own business. Believe me, I'd much rather keep out of your way.

If we do have to live near each other, then I'll happily keep your yards free from lizards, snakes, mice, and creepy-crawlies!

You CAN get rid of skunk smell, but it might be best NOT to spook me into spraying you in the first place. I only spray when I feel THREATENED.

That's my cue to HOP it!

FACTS:

* Skunks have poor eyesight, but they have excellent senses of smell and hearing to make up for it.

* Skunks are omnivores, which means they eat both plants and animals. They like chowing down on fruits, insects, worms, and frogs, and are sometimes even better at catching mice than cats!

* They are very non-aggressive animals, and spraying is the only defense they have against danger.

* Their homes are called dens, which are sometimes built in trees, logs, burrows, and occasionally beneath porches (which gets them into trouble with humans).

You have to admit, I'm pretty COOL-LOOKING. My fashionable stripes are a WARNING to keep away.

We will ALWAYS warn you before spraying. We're just nice like that!

I stomp my feet before I spray. Spotted skunks even do a cute little HANDSTAND! And, honestly, you don't smell so great, either.

What SILLINESS!

We've earned the nickname NATURE'S CLEAN-UP CREW! I hardly ever kill anything—all I'm doing is RECYCLING leftovers. I thought recycling was a GOOD thing—sheesh.

I know I can get a bit possessive of food sometimes, but if I didn't clean up the savanna, there would be SMELLY CARCASSES everywhere. Then you'd really have something to complain about!

FACTS:

* Vultures are vital to the ecosystem. By cleaning up all of the leftovers, they prevent disease from spreading, which stops other animals and people from getting sick.

* When vultures are feeding, they're called a "wake," and when they're flying in a formation, they're called a "kettle." No, not THAT type of kettle!

* The Andean condor, which is a type of vulture, has one of the biggest wingspans of any bird. It measures almost 11.5 feet across, which means that they have enormous feathers!

* When a vulture is upset or annoyed, its whole head turns red, which makes it look like it's blushing.

I'm a RAT

I'll attack anything, so WATCH it!
I scurry and scuttle through the smallest holes, and you won't even hear me coming. There is nowhere to hide from me.
I don't go anywhere without my pals. If you see one of me, then you can be certain my friends are hanging out nearby.
I've got stinky fur, an ugly face, and a BAD attitude.

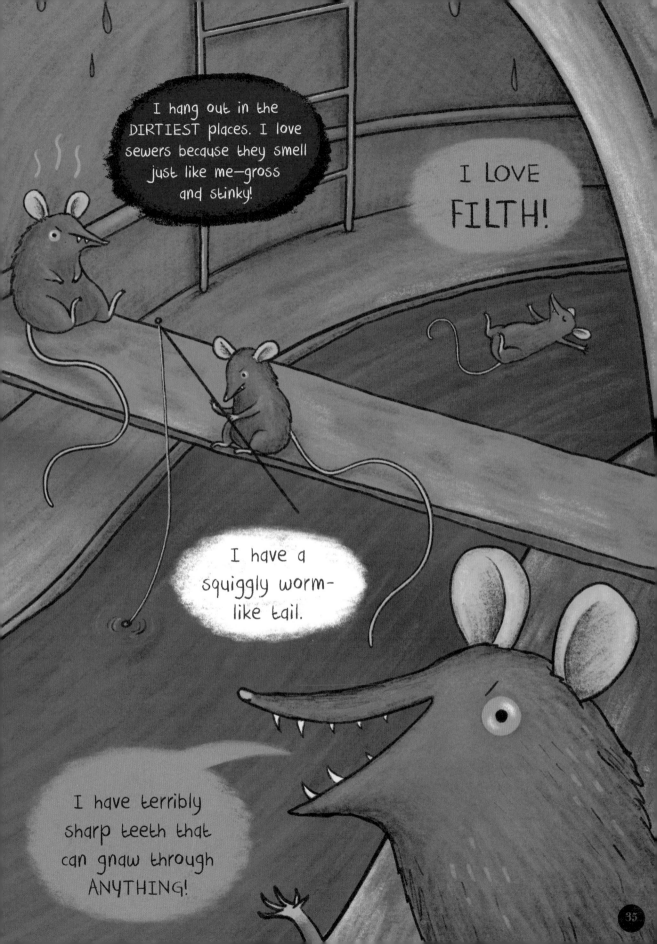

How RIDICULOUS!

I have gorgeous pink ears and eyes like black currants—how could anyone think I was ugly?

I'm a fluffy little SWEETIE!

I only hang out in sewers because I'm shy and I feel SAFE there. But I'll live pretty much anywhere that I can build myself a cozy nest to curl up in. Sometimes I even live in trees.

I'm REALLY smart!

FACTS:

* Rats have really great memories, and scientists have discovered that they can remember human faces they've seen before.

* Some people keep rats as pets. They are very intelligent creatures, can learn tricks very quickly, and love to play with toys!

* A group of rats is called a "mischief." Rats are very social animals and communicate with each other with sounds that can't be heard by the human ear. They also make little chirping noises that sound like human laughter!

* Some wild rats do carry disease, so it's best not to go near them.

I really don't deserve such a FILTHY reputation. I'm actually SQUEAKY clean. I groom myself several times a day! That's even more than you shower. Who's the smelly one now?

Being angry and biting isn't really a hobby of mine. But like most animals, I'll try to defend myself when I feel threatened.

Could I BE any cuter?

I do love gnawing and chewing on things—but that's only because my teeth NEVER stop growing! My teeth can grow up to 4.5 inches a year. I have to keep them in good shape somehow, and I don't have a rat dentist to go to!

That's **SO** unfair!

I'm actually a really useful little critter.

I might have some flaws, but I also gobble up loads of different pests. Without me, there'd be WAY too many creepy-crawlies, and that would be very harmful to our plants.

I'm not really after you—I just wanted a taste of your ice cream! I LOVE sugary things. Please can I have some? Please?

My striking colors are a polite warning for you to keep your distance.

z z z

z z z

It's true I don't make honey, but I do pollinate plants, which makes more lovely flowers grow!

I don't sting people for fun. It's ALWAYS because I feel threatened. People tend to hurt me more than I hurt them.

My cousins the bees are well respected, and we're basically just predatory bees.

Hey, cousin!

Thanks for removing those pesky aphids. We love you, wasp.

I'm more helpful than you realize...

FACTS:

* Wasps help keep crops healthy by getting rid of creatures that eat them. If there were no wasps, farmers would have to use more horrible, harmful pesticides to do their job.

* A wasp sting contains venom. This has a special, scented chemical called a "pheromone" that makes other wasps become more aggressive and likely to sting too. Never swat away a wasp, as they will always try to defend themselves.

* Male wasps are called drones. It's actually only female wasps that are capable of stinging you. OUCH!

* Wasps are rarely aggressive unless you provoke them. It's best to keep away from them if possible, as sometimes just walking in their path can upset them.

I'm a SNAKE

I have a super-weird forked tongue. All the better to HISS at you.

HissSSS!

I'm slithery, slimy, and venomous! One bite from my massive teeth and you're HISTORY.

Sometimes I wrap my slimy body tightly around my prey and SQUEEEEEZE as hard as I can. My muscles are so strong that my prey doesn't stand a chance!

I spend my time waiting for you to step on me so I can bite your ankle. I'm just mean like that.

That's just SSSSILLY!

I'm not AT ALL slimy. My beautiful scaly skin is dry, smooth, and nice and cool to touch!

My eyes aren't scary! They're really very pretty and look like sparkly jewels! I sometimes look like I'm staring, because I don't have eyelids.

My little forked tongue is actually really cute. I flick it to sense where smells are coming from.

Ssssomething sssssmells YUMMY!

I'm not waiting in the grass for you to step on me. That's RIDICULOUS and silly— it really hurts to get stepped on!

It's true that sometimes I do squeeze my prey to stop it running away. This is called "constricting." But we have to eat somehow, guys—nobody likes a rumbly tummy.

FACTS:

* Snakes have flexible jaws that can open incredibly wide. So wide in fact that they can eat things bigger than their own head and can swallow their food whole!

* There are over 3,000 species of snake. They're such a successful group that they live on every continent apart from Antarctica (where it's just too chilly).

* Some snakes pretend to be venomous. The harmless milk snake mimics the colors of the deadly coral snake so that hungry predators will keep away from it.

* Although it might not look like it, snakes do actually have bones in their wriggly, wiggly bodies. They have a long, bendy backbone, which consists of up to 400 spine bones.

Not all snakes are venomous. In fact, only 10% are dangerous to humans.

Rattlesnakes use their rattles as a warning for you to keep away. Quite thoughtful of them, really.

Oh, and I can't hypnotize you. That's just a silly myth.

I'll only bite if I feel THREATENED. So let's all be friends, OK?

I'm a WOLF

I'M BIG. I'M BAD.
And I'm out to GET YOU!

I enjoy making the moon feel uncomfortable when it's full by HOWLING at it.

I hang around with my pack, and we enjoy scaring sheep together. BOO!

I'll pretend to be your grandma...and then I'll EAT you!

Give me a BREAK!

I'm not one to blow my own trumpet, but I AM one of the most beautiful creatures. ON EARTH. I'm ready for my close-up.

I think your howling sounds like music!

AROOOO! Some say my howling is BEAUTIFUL!

FACTS:

* It might sound spooky to us, but wolves actually howl to communicate with each other.

* They can travel up to 50 miles in just one day and can run as fast as 35 miles per hour! That would wear out your sneakers pretty quickly.

* Wolves are very family-orientated and usually stay together in packs of roughly ten individuals, but some packs can include up to thirty animals.

* All pet dogs are related to wolves that were domesticated by humans THOUSANDS of years ago.

Without me, there would be no such thing as a "man's best friend"! All pet dogs are descended from wild wolves. (Although when you see a Chihuahua, it's pretty hard to believe)

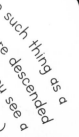

Guys, I'm really not THAT bad!

I'm SMALL but MIGHTY!

In fact, I'm actually good for the environment. Me and my pals break down lots of little bits of waste to keep our world CLEAN!

Honestly, your pants really don't interest me that much. And if I DID crawl in there it was almost certainly an accident. And YOU probably sat on MY nest. So who's to blame really?

I'm trying to LIVE here! Be more careful where you park your butt.

All hail our GRACIOUS queen!

I'm BIG and BEAUTIFUL. You may call me Your Highness.

Our queen ant is the only one of us that lays eggs. And never in your sandwich.

We're really worth knowing about!

It's true I do enjoy sweet foods. But I don't think that makes me a bad ant. I bet you love sweets too! Can you spare a grain of sugar?

FACTS:

* Ants live in a group called a "colony." They work together to find food and bring it back to their queen.

* Some insects only live for a few hours. However, the *Pogonomyrmex owyheei* species of ant can live for up to 30 years!

* They communicate with each other by producing pheromones. These scents tell the ants where to find the best food and act as trails for all the other ants to follow so they don't get lost.

* One single ant can carry something over 50 TIMES their own weight! They also work in pairs or groups to carry heavier leaves and twigs to their nests.

Nice one, team!

We're SO good at teamwork.

53

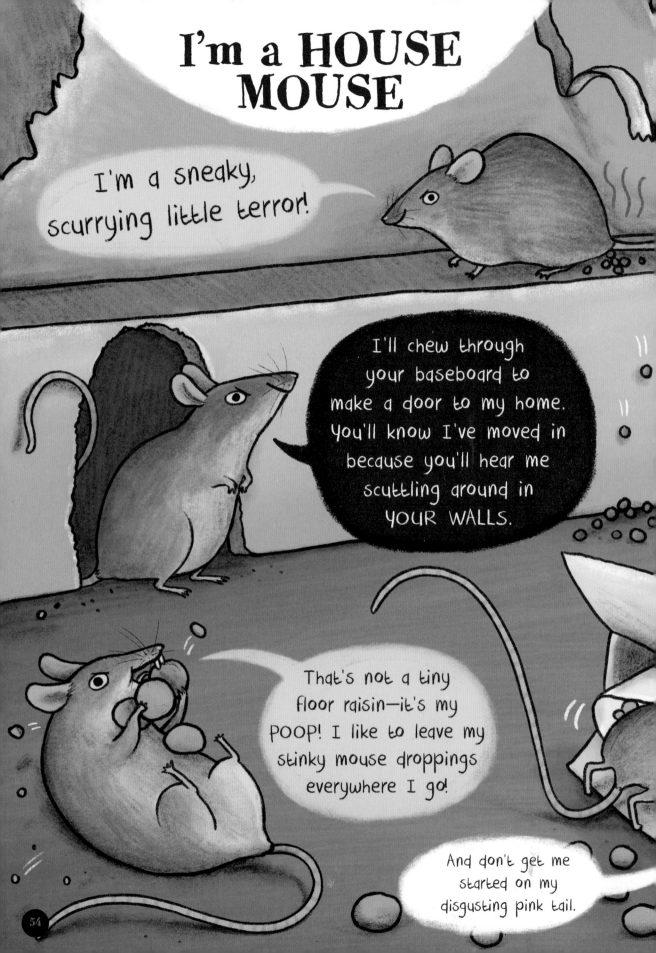

Oh, come <u>ON!</u>

I'm a delightfully tiny, wonderfully fluffy little treasure!

FACTS:

* Most mice are absolutely tiny! They can measure three to four inches long and weigh anywhere from seven to forty grams. They can flatten out their tiny little bodies, which means they can squeeze through tiny gaps—gaps as small as six millimeters!

* Mice use their amazing tails much like a cat does: to balance, feel, and grip. Their tails also help them to climb (which they do astonishingly well) and can grow to the same length as their bodies.

* A mouse's teeth NEVER stop growing, which is why they have to constantly chew things to make sure they don't overgrow.

* There are lots of different species of mice, all with their own unique and wonderful names, including deer mice, wood mice, fancy mice, and even zebra mice!

We might come inside your house, but it's only because we're trying to survive and get some shelter. Mice are on the menu for lots of big animals, so surviving is not always easy for us.

I'm quiet, shy, and a sensitive little sweetheart. Most of us live outside in snuggly little burrows to keep out of danger.

Sometimes we even sleep inside FLOWERS. Possibly the cutest sight you'll ever see!

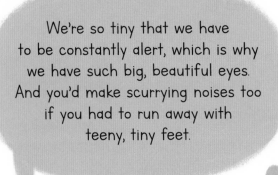

We're so tiny that we have to be constantly alert, which is why we have such big, beautiful eyes. And you'd make scurrying noises too if you had to run away with teeny, tiny feet.

I don't actually squeak often, but when I do, it's ADORABLE.

Oh, and sorry about the poops—I just can't control myself!

So please, if you find me in your house, put me outside and make your house mouse-proof! Your home is just so cozy and that's not MY fault... I just love what you did with the place.

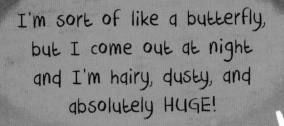

I'm sort of like a butterfly, but I come out at night and I'm hairy, dusty, and absolutely HUGE!

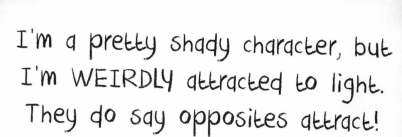

I'm a pretty shady character, but I'm WEIRDLY attracted to light. They do say opposites attract!

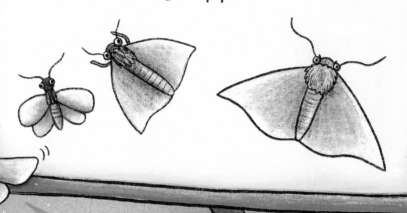

So PRETTY—must TOUCH!

Show me what you're looking at online or I will fly directly into your face.

You couldn't be more WRONG!

I'm sort of like a butterfly. But I'm even better than them because I'm CUDDLY!

Only clothes-moth larvae eat clothes, and they usually only like smelly clothes. So keep your clothes clean and they'll stay hole-free!

I'm not actually DUSTY. My wings have tiny scales on them, which I like to think of as PIXIE DUST.

We're FASCINATING, see?

OMG! Smelly clothes alert! Yum!

FACTS:

* Moths are actually very important pollinators. This helps all of the lovely flowers to produce seeds—we don't usually see the moths, as they're busy pollinating at night.

* Some moths are as small as a tiny little pinhead, while others can grow to be the same size as an adult man's hand!

* Moths seem to be attracted to light because of "transverse orientation." This means that they navigate by the moon, but man-made lights confuse them!

* Some moths have markings on their wings that look like eyes while others have bright flashes of color. These are all defense mechanisms to protect them from being eaten!

Uh-oh!

I don't love light the way humans think. I use the moon to help me find my way around. Artificial lights confuse me...Would you mind switching yours off so I can find my moony friend?

THE MOON

I don't want to brag, but I have the CUTEST fluffy butt around!

I'm FAR from ugly. There's 160,000 different species of moth in the world (though only 17,500 butterfly species), and many of us are very brightly colored and pretty!

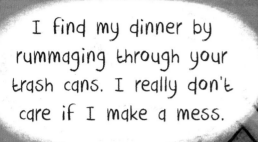

I find my dinner by rummaging through your trash cans. I really don't care if I make a mess.

Who would throw out half a chicken drumstick? Delicious!

I only care about myself. Call me sneaky, sly, cunning. It doesn't matter, I ALWAYS get what I want.

I'm the SNEAKIEST predator on the block. Now where's the chicken coop?

I'm always SCREAMING. Why, I hear you ask? No reason. I just want to CREEP YOU OUT.

63

POPPYCOCK! I'm a truly wonderful little creature.

I'm really not a pest. If food is thrown out in urban areas, then of course I'm going to eat it. It would be a shame to let all that delicious food go to waste.

My ginger fur is BEAUTIFUL! How could anyone think otherwise?

You bet I'm cunning! But my mom always told me being intelligent was a GOOD thing!

What can I say? I'm IRRESISTIBLE!

I'm sorry about making a mess of your trash cans. I'm not doing it to be annoying. But you really shouldn't waste so much food.

Sure, I might have the odd flea, but I'm a WILD animal! It's all part of nature.

Fleas need a home too!

Sorry for SCREAMING so much, I know it can be a bit annoying. But we're just vocal animals. We scream and bark to communicate with other foxes—everyone loves a good chat!

FACTS:

* A female fox is called a "vixen" and a male fox is called a "tod." When they have babies, they are called "pups," "kits," or "cubs." A whole group of foxes is called a "skulk" or a "leash."

* Although foxes are related to dogs, they actually have some characteristics like cats; they retract their claws and have vertical pupils that help them to spot their prey.

* Foxes live in dens. This can be a little hole in the ground that they dig out using their strong paws. Or if the fox lives in the city it might be a cozy spot underneath your shed.

* Foxes have excellent hearing, which helps them out in the wild. This is why they have such lovely large ears.

I usually hunt chickens when I have a litter of cubs to feed. It's my natural instinct to try to feed my babies.

Did somebody say chicken?

Well, that's not TOADally true!

Get your facts straight!

FACTS:

* Toads and frogs are quite similar. The main differences between them are that a toad's legs are shorter, its skin is drier and more bumpy, it can live farther away from water, and it doesn't have any teeth.

* A group of toads is often called a "knot."

* Toads usually come out to hunt at night and hibernate through the cold winter months.

* Toads start out as tiny little tadpoles. When grown, they can live for around ten years in the wild. In captivity, toads have been known to reach 40 years old!

* And no matter what the fairy tales tell you, frogs don't turn into princes either. It's probably best not to kiss any amphibians!

I'm a plump lump of CUTENESS!

I'm not really moody all the time. I only LOOK grumpy, but I can't help what my face looks like! Besides, some people say I'm completely ADORABLE. Look at my huge puppy-like eyes!

Why, HELLO!

Thanks for carrying me, Mom. You're the BEST!

It might seem a bit weird that Surinam toads carry their babies under the skin on their backs. But you can't deny that that's dedicated parenting!

I'm not really a fan of witches. All of their recipes include putting ME in their cauldrons. Um, no thanks!

I might not like swimming, but I DO need water to survive. I like my skin to be moist and not dry.

Unlike jumping frogs, I prefer to walk or take small hops with my cute little legs.

Please don't touch me without washing your hands afterward. I have glands on my skin that carry poison to protect me from predators. But I'm not that dangerous to humans, unless you EAT me—so please don't!

I do catch food with my tongue. But so what? Maybe it's actually YOU that's the weird one for using a knife and fork! Plus, the way I eat means I don't have to do the dishes. Who's laughing now?

I'm a BULL

I'm larger than life, stinkier than a butt, and ALWAYS really angry! Oh, and I can't stop FARTING!

If I see you walking through my field, I'll ATTACK you. Just the thought of it is making me RAGE!

TOOT

toot

I'm really CLUMSY and will smash your best china. Is that your favorite mug? Excuse me while I CRUSH it.

I'm TERRIBLY bad-tempered, and I'll CHARGE at you for no apparent reason. YOU'RE IN FOR IT, PAL!

What NONSENSE!

Sure, I'm pretty HUGE, but I'm quite a clean animal, and I'm absolutely NOT always angry!

Sorry for farting so much. I can't help being gassy! Maybe stay upwind of my bottom burps.

Look at my big, beautiful eyes and cute smile! I'm totally LOVELY.

I'm actually NOT clumsy. For such large animals, we're pretty light on our feet! If you pop around for cup of tea, I promise I won't crush your cup with my big hooves.

I'm really not aggressive. I only get angry when I have to defend myself.

We're more likely to be aggressive if we're left in a field alone because we're social animals. We feel nervous and exposed to danger. Usually, though, we are very docile animals.

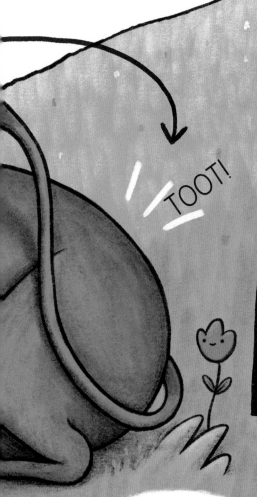

TOOT!

FACTS:

* Bulls are massive, muscular male cows, which are used for breeding.

* They are herbivores and have four chambers in their stomach! These help them break down and digest extra-tough grass and other plants.

* Bulls and cows can get through nearly 45 pounds of food and a bathtub's worth of water every single day! It's no wonder they're so huge.

* Bulls and cows spend a lot of time doing just one thing—chewing! They can chew about 50 times a minute for up to 8 hours a day.

Hooray for bull poop!

My poop is called manure, and it helps flowers grow.

That's nonsense about me hating the color red. I can't even SEE red because I'm color-blind to it!

Phew!

Don't be DAFT!

I'm a gorgeously nimble little fluffster with one of the cutest faces around!

I DO sometimes steal other animals' homes. But I don't do it all the time, and I also dig my own burrows sometimes, too.

I'll admit I go a little overboard with the hunting. I'm just so GOOD at it!

I'll only bite if I get scared or feel threatened. I'll only spray you with stinky butt stuff when I'm terrified. I have to protect myself! So please don't scare me, OK?

Sometimes food is scarce, so even if I'm not very hungry, I'll save food I catch for later. I have a really fast metabolism and heartbeat, so I need lots of food for energy.

Sometimes I dance around for the fun of it! Have you SEEN my disco dancing moves?

Some of us change the color of our fur as the seasons change! I turn white in winter to camouflage myself against the snow. Aren't I pretty?

Wait, what's so confusing about a group of weasels?

Who's calling my tail scraggly? I think you'll find that it is actually ADORABLE. End. Of. Story.

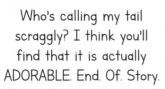

FACTS:

* When weasels turn white in winter they are known as "ermines."

* A group of weasels is sometimes called a "boogle" or "confusion." This is probably because they move so quickly and make bizarre movements that confuse people!

* Weasels are amazing hunters and often prey on creatures much larger than themselves. They have stumpy legs, but their long necks mean they can easily carry bigger prey in their teeth and scurry along at the same time.

* Weasels are very similar in appearance to stoats. The main difference is that stoats have a black tuft of hair at the tip of their tails.

Oh, COME ON...

I'm just a giant awesome lizard!

Food isn't ALL I think about. Sometimes I let birds clean my teeth for me. Thank you, birdy pal, now my teeth are wonderfully shiny again.

Dude, have you been flossing?

FACTS:

* Crocodiles are living dinosaurs. They first appeared 240 MILLION years ago, and saltwater crocodiles are the world's LARGEST living reptiles.

* They have around 65 teeth in their jaws, but don't use them to chew. Instead, they swallow rocks to help them break up what they've eaten. They only use their teeth to grip and crush their prey...Ouch!

* Crocodiles don't sit with their mouths open because they're angry—they're letting off steam! They sweat through their mouths and this is how they cool off.

* Some crocodiles do actually sleep with one eye open! It's called "unihemispheric sleep," which means half of their brain remains alert to danger (or a tasty meal passing nearby)...

Crocs are the coolest!

Because I spend a lot of time basking in the sun, I have bony scales on my back called "scutes." These help me to soak up the sun's rays, and it's just a BONUS that they make me look so cool!

I do spend a lot of my time in the shallows, looking out for my next meal. But just stay away from my hunting area and you'll never be in danger of my super-pointy teeth.

My jaws might be HUGE, but that's because I'm a TOP predator! I should be respected, not feared.

SOMEBODY'S got to be at the top of the food chain, which means us crocs can be pretty aggressive. But our cousins, the alligators, are really chilled out.

Hi there! You can call me Al for short.

That is SO unfair!

I'm basically a DOVE, and people love doves. Why does everyone have a problem with me? I'm just as beautiful!

We won't harass you, but we might watch you eat. Your food just looks so tasty. Are you going to finish that sandwich?

We don't CHOOSE to eat trash. But it's readily available to us in places where people live. We pick up what YOU drop! There wouldn't be so many of us if people weren't so wasteful.

Look at my pretty plumage!

And check out my cute pink toes!

I don't just walk around, I STRUT! Love me for my sassy walk, if nothing else.

I don't INFEST towns and cities!
I just happen to live there—
just like you! There are lots of
different types of pigeon that live
in all kinds of places, including
cliff faces, woodland, and forests.
We're not just city slickers!

Some people think that when birds
poop on your head it is a sign of
GOOD luck! So, um, you're welcome.
But maybe take a shower.

I'm a great
postman!

I don't carry diseases,
but my poop can if
there's too much of
it. But whose poop is
squeaky clean anyway?

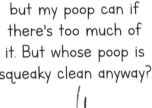

FACTS:

* There are over 300 different species of pigeon, and they can be found all over the world. Although they're not particularly fond of deserts, they can be found in rain forests, grasslands, savannas, mangrove swamps, and rocky areas.

* Pigeons have an exceptional sense of direction. They even carried important messages back and forth during World Wars I and II. They're war heroes!

* They have a keen sense of hearing. Pigeons can hear low-frequency sounds that we can't hear and so are able to detect distant storms and earthquakes.

* Pigeons are actually very intelligent birds. Scientists say that they can recognize themselves in the mirror and can even tell apart all the letters in the alphabet!

I'm a CAMEL

I'm a grumpy beast, and as you can tell by my face, NOTHING impresses me.

I have a lumpy, bumpy, humpy back covered in shaggy, dirty hair. Try and ride me and you'll be in for the bumpiest journey of your life.

I grunt and grumble ALL the time. Grruuumble.

I store water in my weird back hump so I can practice SPITTING all day and don't have to stop for a drink. Obviously.

I'm massively stinky and PROUD of it.

Are you having a <u>LAUGH</u>?

I do grumble and grunt a lot, but I promise my heart is in the right place. People ask me to do a lot of things, and to be fair, I do it all. But I reserve the right to moan about it as I do it!

You WISH you had eyelashes as long as mine!

I am actually impressed by some things. It's just that I can't express it with my face. But I've been known to jump for joy when I'm given a tasty treat! Mmm—delicious!

I don't actually like spitting, but it usually stops people annoying me. I only spit if I feel threatened or really bothered by something. So basically, just don't annoy me and I'll keep my saliva to myself.

I might be a bit stinky, but surprisingly, I rarely sweat!

Food is super hard to find in the desert. It's not actually water in my humps—it's where I store fat so that I have a reserve of food and energy for when I can't find a tasty shrub or cactus.

Most of my kind live in the desert, but we're perfectly adapted to the hot climate and don't mind it one bit! The sun is my friend.

Hi, pal!

FACTS:

* There are two species of camel in the world; the dromedary camel, which only has one hump, and the bactrian camel, which has two humps.

* Camels are perfectly adapted for the hot and sandy desert life. Their feet are big and wide, which means they don't sink into the sand when they walk. They also have gorgeously long eyelashes that keep the sand out of their eyes. Their nostrils also work to keep sand away by closing up when necessary.

* They have lived and worked alongside humans for over 5,000 years. Because they are so strong and reliable on sandy terrain, they have earned the nickname "ships of the desert."

All aboard the SS Camel!

89

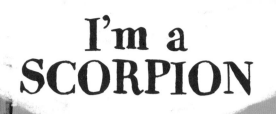

I'm a
SCORPION

I'm like something from a terrible dream. But when you wake up, I'M STILL THERE.

I have eight scuttling legs and two terrifying PINCERS. I scurry around the desert, pinching and stinging anything in my path!

I'm totally indestructible and POISONOUS. I mean, come on, just look at me! OF COURSE I'm poisonous!

Come on now! I'm not <u>THAT</u> bad.

In fact, I'm here to tell you that I'm pretty cute. Yes, you heard me, CUTE.

I'm not indestructible. But I am a survivor! I don't need to eat very often and my armor protects me from harsh conditions. Actually my life span is pretty short. We only live for around five years in the wild. So if you'll excuse me, I've got to go and do some carefree scuttling!

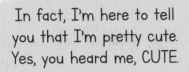

I'm not poisonous, but I am a bit venomous (meaning my venom has to be injected to cause any harm). However, it's actually only a few species of scorpions that can cause real harm to humans.

Cute tiny stinger, NOT a massive needle.

I only sting with the little pointy bit at the end of my tail. This is called a "stinger," and I only use it if I'm feeling threatened or when I'm hunting. Usually I'll just run away and hide or pinch and grab at things adorably with my pincers.

92

FACTS:

* There are about 2,000 different species of scorpion, each one more fascinating than the last. They vary greatly in size—the biggest is almost 8 inches long and the smallest is only about 9 millimeters long. Aww!

* Scorpions are nocturnal creatures, which means they usually come out at night. Some species actually spend almost their entire lives in burrows underground!

* Incredibly, scorpions can survive for up to a YEAR without food! They slow down their metabolism when food is scarce.

* Scorpions molt their body armor as they grow up. This can happen up to seven times to reach their adult size. For the first few hours after molting, they are more vulnerable to danger because their new skin is soft and delicate at first, but gradually hardens.

My babies are called scorplings. That has to be one of the cutest words in the English language.

I'm actually pretty majestic if you look at my properly, take the time to get to know me, and don't judge me right away. I'm perfectly adapted to where I live and I actually GLOW in the dark because of UV fluorescence.

We are CREEPY BIRDS

We're fiendish and feathered and our purpose in life is to CREEP you out.

I'm a crow and love showing up in the SPOOKIEST of places.

Your pitiful "scarecrows" won't keep me away.

CAWWW

A group of crows is called a MURDER. Need I say more?

Don't be so SUPERSTITIOUS!

We're the COOLEST birds around...

FACTS:

* Crows, magpies, and ravens are just some of the brilliant birds that are part of the Corvidae family. There are over 120 types of corvid species.

* Corvids are actually very playful birds and use their intelligence and excellent mimicry skills to communicate and play games with each other. They sometimes even play pranks on humans!

* They are very family-orientated and sensitive creatures. Scientists have discovered that they can remember if a human does a good deed for them. They have even been known to bring gifts to people who feed them.

* Legend has it that ravens have been kept in the Tower of London since the time of King Charles II (1600–1685). At least six ravens must remain at the tower, or the monarchy and Britain will fall.

Scarecrows won't keep me away because I'm incredibly smart—not because I'm mean! Farmers don't want us eating their crops, but we have to eat too and sometimes their produce is just too tasty to miss.

I know it sounds spooky, but "murder" is just the word used to describe a group of us. That's all there is to it, and it was actually humans who named us, so who's the creepy one now?

96

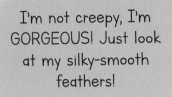

Wait a second!
You've got it all WRONG!

Killer whale isn't even my real name! I'm an ORCA, and I'm not even a whale! I'm actually part of the dolphin family.

I'm not a bully or bad tempered! I have smooth skin and such a sweet little smile! How could you be scared of this face?

It's true that we hunt in packs, but this shouldn't be something to fear— it's something to celebrate! It takes A LOT of brains and clever communication to do this, which means we're SUPER smart.

Baby orcas look just like miniature versions of their parents. Orca pods (families) are very tight-knit, and they tend to stick together as the calves grow up.

I'm a picky eater, but humans are not my go-to meal! I'm really in the mood for a walrus salad, though...

We're too intelligent, big, and majestic to be kept in tanks. We need freedom to roam and stretch our wonderful strong bodies!

FACTS:

* Killer whales (or orcas) have been swimming around our great big planet for roughly 11 MILLION years—much longer than us humans! So really, we should be thanking them for letting us share the planet with them.

* Orcas can grow up to more than 30 feet long and are the biggest species of dolphin in the world. And they have a HUGE appetite to match their size. They can eat around 500 pounds of food in just one day!

* Orcas live in groups called pods. Each pod communicates and navigates differently. Scientists have discovered that they even seem to have their own distinct "cultures" varying from pod to pod.

* These creatures will eat everything from seals to sea lions, penguins, squid, sea turtles, and even sharks and whales!

Oh, that's just RIDICULOUS!

FACTS:

* There are more than 200 different species of jellyfish around the world, and they've been around for roughly 500 MILLION years! They were even here before the dinosaurs!

* Some jellyfish are bioluminescent, which means they can produce their own light!

* Weirdly, jellyfish don't have a brain, heart, bones, or eyes!

* Because of their bag-like bodies, some sea creatures that eat jellyfish, such as sea turtles, have mistaken discarded plastic bags for their jelly dinner. It's important to keep our oceans clean, as they have an effect on all life on Earth.

It's true that I'm pretty wibbly and wobbly, but I definitely WON'T chase you. If I sting you, it's always by accident. Just don't get in my jolly jelly way and you'll be fine.

Peeing on a sting doesn't help. Don't be weird, dude.

Always recycle!

I'm an ultra-cool, fascinating, and beautiful creature—almost like something from outer space! How awesome is that?

Some jellies do contain a really dangerous venom that is deadly to humans, but for the most part we're really very harmless.

To be safe, it's probably best not to touch us, though!

Jellyfish babies are TINY and so cute! Just call me a jelly baby.

If you see one of my kind on the beach, then very sadly it's because we've passed away. But even so, don't touch our tentacles because they can still sting.

I'm a DUNG BEETLE

You won't believe how utterly DISGUSTING I am. I bet you can't guess what my most FAVORITE thing is...

POOP!

If loving poop wasn't bad enough, then check out my weird horns and my super-fluttery wings.

Yes, you heard me right. POOP!

I like to gather up as much poop as I can and roll around huge balls of it.

Oh dear...

I hate to break it to you, but I really do eat poop. But I promise you it's not really all that weird—I'm just recycling waste.

One creature's poop is a dung beetle's DINNER!

Us dung beetles work together. Some dung beetles ROLL poop, some TUNNEL into it, and others just LIVE on it. It's a handy resource for us.

Don't judge me for my unique taste. Everyone likes different things. And definitely don't judge me for my AMAZING horns and SUPER-COOL wings. I think they make me look pretty snazzy!

Chimps, rabbits, and even dogs have been known to eat dung—I just get a bad name for it because that's all I eat!

I'll either eat the dung or lay eggs in it—either way it's better than it going to waste!

Thanks for cleaning up, pal!

No problem, buddy.

The coolest thing about me is that relative to my size I'm the STRONGEST animal on EARTH!

FACTS:

* Dung beetles have existed for roughly 30 million years. We know this because scientists have uncovered huge fossilized dung balls from that period of time.

* There are three main kinds of dung beetle: rollers, tunnelers, and dwellers. Rollers shape the poop into balls and roll them away; tunnelers dig through the balls; and dwellers just live inside the pile of poop! They also use their balls of poop to cool off in the hot desert sun. Sand in the desert gets very hot, so the beetles protect their feet by standing on the cool dung instead of the hot sand.

* Although their name might suggest it, poop isn't the only thing that dung beetles care about. They are one of the few groups of insects that care for their young and some dung beetle couples stay together for life!

I'm a CENTIPEDE

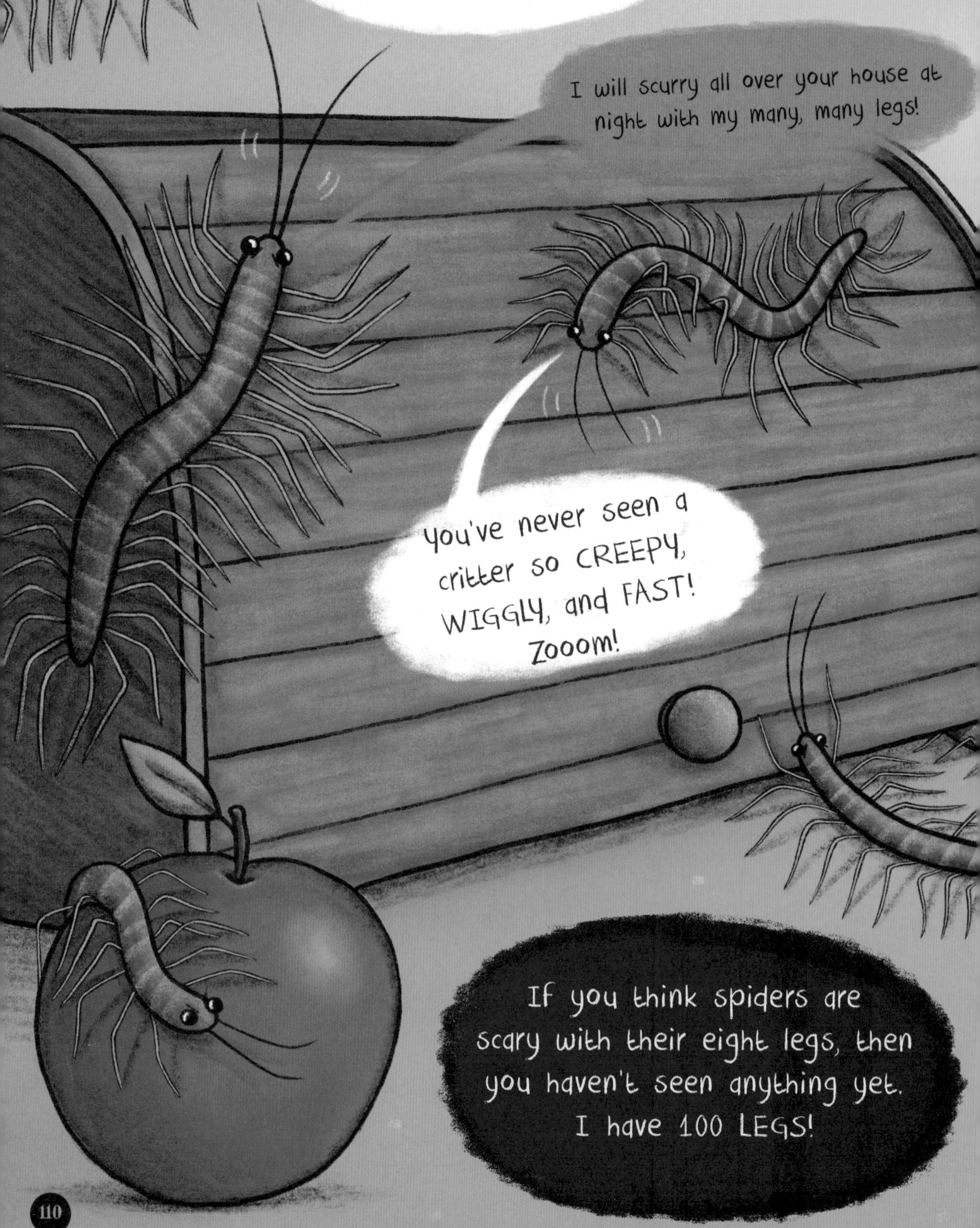

What SILLINESS!

I'm a leggy little friend, not foe!

I'm a house centipede. I don't actually have 100 legs. That's just a silly myth. I really only have around 30-40, which might look a bit strange to you, but you really shouldn't judge someone because they look different from you.

They help me run super fast. And you must admit, they make me look pretty cool.

I'm also pretty helpful. I keep your house free from bugs that you really don't want scurrying around, like bedbugs, termites, and cockroaches.

Lots of my kind live outdoors and gardeners love us because we aerate (which means we add air to) the soil. This helps keep plants healthy.

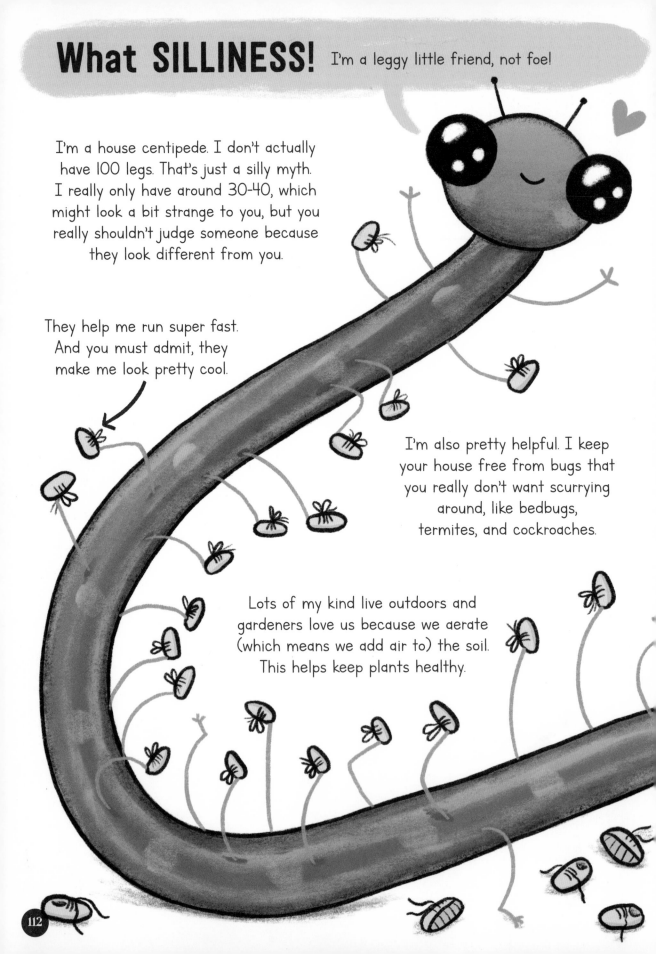

FACTS:

*   There are thought to be around 8,000 species of centipede. They're actually one of the oldest groups of animals in the world, and they first appeared on planet Earth roughly 430 MILLION years ago!

*   They live all over the planet in lots of different habitats. From tropical rain forests and wooded forests to hot and sandy deserts and even near the Arctic Circle.

*   Centipedes are predators, meaning they hunt other creatures. However, they are also prey and have to be careful that they don't become someone else's dinner! They can detach (and re-grow) some of their legs to escape being eaten.

*   Despite their name meaning "hundred legs," no centipede actually has exactly 100 legs! They can have between 30 and an incredible 354! Imagine how stressful shoe shopping would be!

I'm not filthy at all! I'm actually a really clean little bug. I don't make webs or nests, and I spend lots of time cleaning my many lovely legs to make sure they're all in tip-top condition.

I'm basically harmless to humans. I'll only bite you if you handle me, so just leave me be and I'll be the perfect roommate.

SO WHAT if I'm slimy? I'm a miraculous little mollusk!

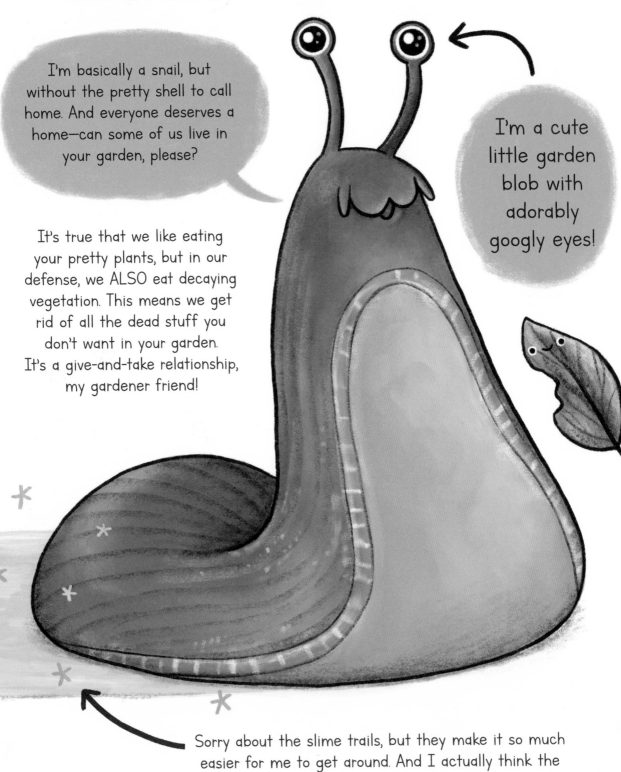

I'm basically a snail, but without the pretty shell to call home. And everyone deserves a home—can some of us live in your garden, please?

I'm a cute little garden blob with adorably googly eyes!

It's true that we like eating your pretty plants, but in our defense, we ALSO eat decaying vegetation. This means we get rid of all the dead stuff you don't want in your garden. It's a give-and-take relationship, my gardener friend!

Sorry about the slime trails, but they make it so much easier for me to get around. And I actually think the way they shimmer is quite pretty!

Gardeners need to understand that us gastropods (slugs and snails) are part of a healthy ecosystem that will make their garden thrive in the long run. For a start, lots of adorable animals like hedgehogs and birds rely on us to be their dinner.

Well, hello there, good-looking!

FACTS:

* There are around 5,000 species of slug crawling around the world. They love living in damp and cool places and need to stay moist to survive.

* Slugs have a good sense of smell and can actually detect smells with their tentacles! They also follow the scent of their mucus trails to find their way back to their tunnels or to follow other slugs to tasty plants.

* They are omnivores and help keep soil healthy by eating rotting leaves and animal remains and pooping it back into the wild!

* Amazingly, slugs can stretch to 20 times their normal length! This helps them get into tiny gaps to reach food.

I'm really rather fascinating if you take the time to learn about me. I'm basically a "stomach foot" (that's what gastropod means) covered in a bit of mucus.

We come in all sorts of lovely colors, and there's even a type of sea slug that looks just like a little bunny!

Hi there. You can call me Sloppy Hoppy.

That's some serious stretching!

I'm an ANGLERFISH

I'm the UGLIEST fish around, and I lurk in the deepest, darkest depths of the ocean. It's so dark down here that it's almost impossible to see anything.

But wait, what's that? Why it's a tasty, wiggly worm! Come and get your dinner, little fishy!

I have horribly wonky, super-sharp teeth. All the better to bite you with!

AHA! It's NOT a worm! It's my jiggly, wiggly, glowing FISHING LINE! And you've been well and truly HOOKED!

I'm a HUGE, sneaky monster of the deep, fooling unsuspecting creatures into becoming MY DINNER!

Am I here? Am I there? You won't see me coming when I chase you through the dark water!

I'll be waiting for you to swim by...

Hold on a second! Let me throw some LIGHT on the situation.

I think you'll find that I'm actually a ridiculously cool-looking WONDER of nature!

I won't chase you. In fact, I'm such a slow swimmer, I couldn't even if I tried.

Stop thinking I'm a huge, terrible monster! Most of my kind are actually pretty small. Usually less than a foot long.
Now that's really not so scary, is it?

I'm just a little fish that loves to go about my own business and catch my dinner in my own delightfully different way.

Don't be JEALOUS of my special built-in glowing fish lure. We can't all look this snazzy.

I won't hurt you unless you're a tasty crustacean. Are you a crustacean? No? Well then, let's be FRIENDS!

I'm UNIQUE and should be celebrated!

FACTS:

* There are more than 200 species of anglerfish, most of which live deep in the Atlantic and Arctic Oceans and can survive over half a mile below the water's surface.

* Only female deep-sea anglerfish have a special luminescent lure on their heads. The males of the species are actually much smaller and have even been known to hitch a ride on the females. They rely on female anglerfish to catch their dinner for them. Girl power!

* An anglerfish can light up its lure thanks to tiny glowing bacteria in it.

* Anglerfish have huge mouths to help them swallow their prey. Scientists have discovered that they can eat things twice as large as their body size! They must have a huge appetite!

Don't judge me because I'm a bit ugly—don't you know beauty is on the inside?

I have seen wonders of the deep blue sea that humans couldn't even DREAM of. If you're nice to me, I might show you where you can find a new species of fish...

You couldn't be more WRONG!

I'm a total sweetie pie!
How could you NOT love me?

My fur isn't filthy at all. In fact, it's nice and clean. I look after myself very well, and if a horrid tick creeps onto me, I'll get rid of it right away!

If you leave food out, well then, OF COURSE I'll eat it. But my eating habits are actually really useful because I eat pests like ticks too. So really, I'm not bad to have in your garden.

Please can I stay?

FACTS:

* Despite looking like giant rodents, opossums are the USA and Canada's only marsupial (pouched mammals). This means that they're actually more closely related to kangaroos than to rats.

* Opossums have "prehensile" tails. This means that they can use them as an extra arm. They can hang from branches and even carry things with them.

* They are nocturnal animals, which means that they mostly hunt at night. However, they have really poor eyesight, so they depend a lot on their sense of smell while hunting.

* Opossums are peaceful animals but will growl or "play dead" if they are cornered or feel threatened. Most animals avoid eating carrion, so will leave them alone. They can stay in their pretend dead position for around four hours!

Guys, you're barking up the wrong tree!

Pit bulls were actually bred to be good, loyal companions to humans.

Dogs like us can be VERY misunderstood. I know we can sometimes be scary-LOOKING but we're really very sweet if you take the chance to get to know us.

All breeds of dogs can be sweet and friendly, and all breeds of dogs have the potential to be very mischievous and mean. This depends a lot on how they are trained and raised as puppies.

If we're treated badly by humans, we can turn into nasty dogs. But if we're treated nicely, loved, and given lots of attention, then we'll turn out nice!

This guy could be barky and bitey.

And this guy could be cuddly and gentle.

I don't like wearing spiked collars. I prefer FLUFFY ones.

Throw the ball?

FACTS:

* Many large dog breeds are given a bad reputation because of how they look and their size. Some of these misunderstood breeds include pit bulls, Staffordshire bull terriers, Doberman pinschers, German shepherds, and rottweilers. However, all of them can actually make great family pets.

* German shepherds are often used as working dogs by the police and help them to fight crime. They're too busy with their important jobs to care what some people might say about them!

* Some dogs do not feel comfortable with people coming up to them. Always treat pets with respect and ask the owner before petting a dog.

* Dogs that have come from bad homes can be rehabilitated—they just need love.

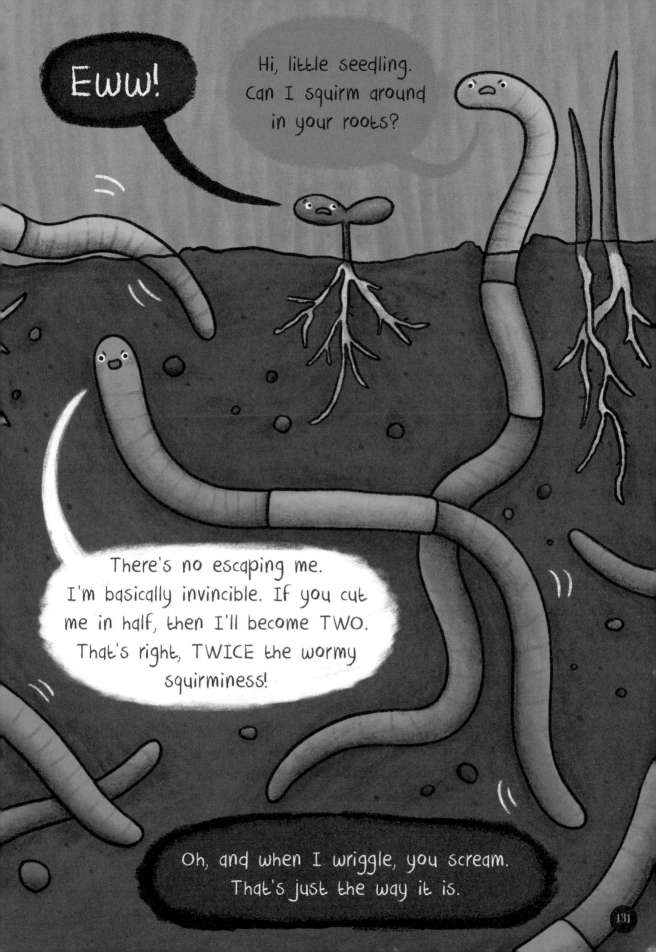

You guys are SO judgmental.

Cute critters love to eat me because I'm SO nutritious and juicy! It's a health hazard for me, but I help keep the world turning and I'm A-OK with that!

Sure, I wiggle and jiggle and dig all day long, but is that a bad thing? I LOVE it! Maybe you should try it someday—it's actually a lot of fun!

I'm a BOOKworm! Reading is the coolest.

FACTS:

* There are around 6,000 species of earthworm in the world, inhabiting every continent except Antarctica. They are as old as dinosaurs and first wriggled into existence around 200 million years ago!

* They are very sensitive to light and can become paralyzed if they stay in the sun too long. They much prefer the cozy, earthy darkness, so if you see a worm out in the sun, make sure to rescue it by putting it on some shaded grass.

* Worms have five hearts! Their hearts are single-chambered, unlike human hearts, which have four chambers.

* Australia is home to one of the longest species of worm—the Gippsland giant earthworm. Amazingly, they can grow up to 10 feet long! You'd definitely notice if you saw one of those wriggling around in your garden.

I'm a KOMODO DRAGON

The clue is in the name. I'm a hugely ferocious, completely deadly DRAGON!

I'll breathe fire on you if you get in my bad books. So, WATCH IT, buddy!

My slobbery saliva is poisonous and so deadly that it will MELT through anything with just one single drop!

I'm a dim-witted, lumbering, huge lump of a creature.

Guys, let me tell you a thing or two about all that NONSENSE.

I'm not really a dragon.

Well, I AM, but not the kind in fairy tales. I can't breathe flames and set fire to villages, I don't have big scaly wings, and I definitely don't steal princesses.

I'm more of a lizard than anything, and I'm actually pretty darn intelligent. Oh, and don't let my super-awesome size deceive you, I'm a VERY fast sprinter when I need to be.

That's silliness about my saliva. I'll have you know that it is perfectly normal and poison-free!

However, I do have a venomous bite. This means the venom is only harmful if I bite something. It's probably best not to go anywhere near my mouth. Nobody is perfect!

PHEW!

I can only really climb trees when I'm small because as an adult I grow to be pretty big.

FACTS:

* Komodo dragons are the largest lizards in the world and can grow to be up to 10 feet long and weigh over 300 pounds.

* They are very rare and are only found on a handful of small islands in the wild, including the Komodo National Park and the island of Flores.

* Amazingly, Komodo dragons can create offspring without the help of a mate! This is called asexual reproduction.

* Komodo dragons have actually been known to play tug-of-war and respond playfully to rubber rings and shoes!

Look at these chubby little claws—CUTE!

I'm a carnivore, which means that I like eating meat. It's true that I'm a pretty fierce hunter, but I also eat a lot of animals that have already passed away, which cleans up the environment.

That's all WRONG!

First of all, I can't even sweat!

But I can burn, and lovely mud all over my skin actually helps to protect me against the hot sun.

FACTS:

* Pigs are considered the fifth most intelligent animal in the world; even more intelligent than cats and dogs!

* Mothers have a special squeal that they use to let their newborn piglets know that it's time to eat. The piglets learn to recognize this and when called come running to their mother!

* Despite having a reputation for being dirty, pigs are actually one of the cleanest farm animals. They don't have sweat glands, so they like to wallow in mud because it helps to cool them down and regulates their body temperature.

* They're definitely not lazy! They snuffle around constantly, and an adult pig can run roughly 11 miles in just one hour!

Mud is so much FUN to wallow in! Have you ever tried it? You're missing out if you haven't!

I'm actually super clean (apart from the mud). And I always make sure to poop far away from where I live.

I make CUTE noises like OINK and have an adorable squishy nose and curly-whirly tail!

Whoever came up with the phrase "eat like a pig" clearly never saw a pig eating. We actually eat slowly and carefully. So THERE.

I'm actually not grumpy at all! I'm one of the sweetest animals around. Want a cuddle?

There aren't many things in the world lovelier than a piglet!

I won't use my ink without a reason, and I usually only use it to protect myself. It confuses predators, which means that I can make a quick getaway!

Hey, deep-sea cousin!

FACTS:

* There are 300 known species of squid in the world. They are invertebrates (which means they don't have a backbone) and mollusks (which means they're related to snails!).

* Squid have three hearts! That must be why they're so lovely.

* They are the world's largest (and most intelligent!) invertebrates. Giant and colossal squid can both grow to more than 40 feet long and have eyes that are as big as basketballs. This is larger than any other known animal!

* Along with squirting ink, squid often use camouflage or bright patterns to deter predators. Some can even become almost transparent to help them blend into their surroundings.

Sure, I can grow quite big, but since when is that a bad thing? Personally, I think it's pretty awesome.

You haven't seen me, right?

Guys, us gulls really AREN'T all that bad!

I don't JUST eat fries. I do a lot of my own hunting for fish and clean up other tasty morsels that wash up on the beach.

We love food, and when you feed us treats at the seaside, it confuses us. How are we supposed to know when you DON'T want us to take your tasty snacks?

So really you shouldn't have fed us your fries in the first place... they're YUMMY but NOT good for us.

I do a groovy little stomping dance to charm worms up from the soil! The worms think it's raining so pop up to see what's going on.

What did he just say?

I think he said he wants to have lunch with us!

FACTS:

* Seagulls can be found all over the world. Fluttering through busy city streets, soaring over big blue oceans, and even in the freezing cold Arctic and Antarctica.

* They are very intelligent birds and have figured out lots of clever ways to find food. This includes stamping their feet to imitate rainfall to encourage earthworms to the surface and breaking mollusks open by dropping them onto rocks!

* Seagulls use many calls and movements to communicate with each other and make fantastic, caring parents to their baby chicks.

* Unlike most animals, seagulls can drink saltwater without getting sick! They get rid of the salt through their nostrils, shaking their head to spray the salty drops off the end of the bill.

We want to be in a trash can!

Eating trash isn't much fun. Please don't litter, and we won't have a problem.

It's good luck when a bird poops on you or your head! The more birds that do, the LUCKIER (or smellier?) you will be!

I'm a SNAPPING TURTLE

I'm an awful grouch, and I'll snap your finger off in one go!

You expect me to be slow because I'm a turtle, but just you wait until you see my super-speedy SNAP! SNAP, SNAP!

What SILLINESS!

I'm an adorable, prehistoric-looking, shy little snapper!

I'm quite chilled and content while I'm in the water, but get pretty grumpy if I'm on land. I just don't like being out of my comfort zone!

Unlike most turtles, I can't hide in my shell for defense, so I have to be on guard. Sorry if that makes me seem a little grouchy sometimes, but I'm just looking out for myself.

I'm an interesting little fella!

As a snappy little predator, I'm important because I keep populations of other animals in balance.

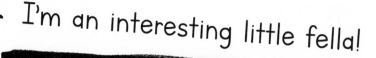

FACTS:

* Snapping turtles spend most of their time in water, usually in lakes and ponds. However, they go on land to lay their eggs in sandy soil.

* Because their tongues are fixed in their heads, they have to eat underwater so the food will move around to allow it to be chewed.

* The alligator snapping turtle has a worm-like lure on the end of its tongue, which it wiggles to entice fish to come closer so it can catch them!

* The Australian white-throated snapping turtle is nicknamed "the butt-breathing turtle." It can breathe almost 70% of its oxygen through its bottom!

'Ello there!

My mom laid 40 of us.

I lay perfectly round little eggs. Look how CUTE they are!

Excuse me, I'm a Tasmanian CUTIE!

There's nothing devilish about me.

FACTS:

* Wild Tasmanian devils are native to Tasmania (surprise, surprise!) in Australia. They are the world's largest (and probably most awesome) carnivorous marsupials but only grow up to 2.5 feet tall.

* Females carry their young in little pouches. They have enough room for four tiny babies at one time. Adorably, baby Tasmanian devils are called joeys or imps!

* Along with getting an unfair name, Tasmanian devils have had a rough time from humans. They were hunted almost to extinction in the late 1800s, but thankfully in 1941 the government introduced new laws to protect them.

* Tasmanian devils travel long distances, up to 10 miles, each night to find food.

I admit I get a little carried away when eating sometimes, but that's only because I LOVE food!

I'm small but SASSY. Us miniature creatures have to stand our ground in this world—don't shame me for it!

Check out my sweet little whiskers!

Glossary

Agile – can move quickly and easily

Amphibian – a family of animals that includes frogs, toads, and newts

Aphid – a small bug that feeds by sucking sap from plants

Aquatic – an animal that lives in water

Arachnid – a family of animals that includes spiders, scorpions, and ticks

Bacteria – tiny living things. Some of them can make you sick, but most animals also depend on them to survive.

Camouflage – when an animal has colors or patterns that make it difficult for you to spot

Carcass – the body of a dead animal

Carnivore – an animal that just eats meat

Carrion – an animal that is already dead, instead of one that another animal has hunted to eat

Climate – the kind of weather that a place usually has. This could be hot or cold, dry or rainy.

Communicate – how animals talk to each other. Sometimes this is by making sounds, but sometimes it is through movements or smells.

Continent – a big area of land made up of lots of countries

Crops – plants that farmers grow for us to eat

Crustacean – a family of animals that includes crabs, lobsters, and shrimp

Digit – a finger or toe

Docile – calm and peaceful

Domestic – an animal that lives in a house with a family, not in the wild

Ecosystem – how all the animals and plants in a place are connected and depend on each other

Environment – the natural world, including plants and animals

Flexible – bendy

Food chain – a way of showing which animals hunt each other to eat. The animal at the top of the food chain doesn't get hunted by anyone.

Formation – a shape that a flock of birds make when they all fly together

Fossil – the remains of a plant or animal from a long time ago. You can sometimes find these in rocks.

Gland – a part of an animal that makes a specific liquid, like sweat or sometimes even poison

Groom – how animals clean themselves

Habitat – the place where an animal lives. This could be a desert, a rain forest, or the sea.

Heat sensor – a part of an animal that tells it when it's touching something hot

Herbivore – an animal that just eats plants

Insect – a family of animals that includes ants, wasps, and beetles

Instinct – how an animal knows what to do to survive. It might have an instinct for how to hunt or how to protect itself.

Larvae – baby insects

Lens – a part of the eye that helps animals see

Low-frequency – deep sounds, sometimes too deep for humans to hear

Luminescent – glowing

Lure – a part of an anglerfish's body, shaped a bit like a fishing rod, that lights up or looks like food. It tempts other fish to swim close so it can eat them.

Mammal – a family of animals that includes dogs, elephants, and people

Marsupial – a kind of mammal that carries its babies in a pouch

Metabolism – how an animal's body gets energy from food

Mimic – copy

Mollusk – a family of animals that includes snails, slugs, and oysters

Molt – when an animal sheds its fur, skin, or feathers so a new one can grow

Mucus – a slime that slugs and snails use to help them slide along

Navigating – finding your way

Nutritious – when food has lots of goodness in it

Offspring – babies

Omnivore – an animal that eats plants and meat

Paralyzed – when you can't move

Pest – an animal that harms plants or other animals

Pesticide – a chemical that farmers use to get rid of pests

Pheromone – a natural chemical that animals give off to communicate with each other through smell

Pincers – a scorpion's sharp claws, which open and close

Plumage – a bird's feathers

Poison – something that could make you sick if you touch or eat it

Pollinate – how plants reproduce. When insects feed inside flowers, their legs pick up a sticky powder called pollen. When they move on to the next flower, the pollen brushes off their legs and helps the plant to make new plants.

Population – how many of a particular animal live in an area

Predator – an animal that hunts other animals for food

Prehistoric – from a long, long time ago, like the dinosaurs

Prey – an animal that is hunted by other animals for food

Pupil – the black part of an animal's eye

Rehabilitate – working with an animal so it can learn to be friendly to humans

Retract – draw back. Cats and foxes can do this with their claws so they don't scratch.

Rodent – a family of animals that includes rats, mice, and guinea pigs

Rotate – turn around, like spinning on the spot

Saliva – an animal's spit

Scavenger – an animal that steals food other animals have hunted, instead of hunting for itself

Species – a kind of animal. A mouse is a different species from a spider, but there are also lots of different kinds of mouse and spider.

Territory – the bit of land where an animal lives and feeds. Some animals will chase others away from their territory.

Transparent – see-through, like a window

Venom – a type of poison that can make you sick if an animal bites or stings you

Wingspan – the distance from the tip of one wing to the other

Further Reading

Want to find out more about the amazing world of animals? Check out these creature feature books!

The Animal Awards

By Martin Jenkins and Tor Freeman
Celebrate the most spectacular species in the animal kingdom and read all about 50 fantastic creatures who are awarded prizes to celebrate their most dazzling talents and some unusual skills.

What Do Animals Do All Day?

By Wendy Hunt and Studio Muti
What *do* animals do all day? Find out in this fully illustrated book that features more than 100 animals.

Encyclopedia of Animals

By Jules Howard and Jarom Vogel
Plunge into the diversity of the animal kingdom, packed with over 500 creatures.

Inspiring | Educating | Creating | Entertaining

Brimming with creative inspiration, how-to projects, and useful information to enrich your everyday life, Quarto Knows is a favorite destination for those pursuing their interests and passions. Visit our site and dig deeper with our books into your area of interest: Quarto Creates, Quarto Cooks, Quarto Homes, Quarto Lives, Quarto Drives, Quarto Explores, Quarto Gifts, or Quarto Kids.

First Published in 2020 by Frances Lincoln Children's Books,
an imprint of The Quarto Group.
400 First Avenue North, Suite 400, Minneapolis, MN 55401, USA.
T (612) 344-8100 F (612) 344-8692 **www.QuartoKnows.com**

A catalog record for this book is available from the British Library.

ISBN 978-0-7112-4748-2

The Illustrations were created digitally
Set in DK Crayon Crumble and Letters for Learners

Published by Katie Cotton and Georgia Amson-Bradshaw
Designed by Andrew Watson
Edited by Claire Grace
Consultant Barbara Taylor
Production by Nicolas Zeifman

Manufactured in Guangdong, China CC012020
9 8 7 6 5 4 3 2 1